Francis Creek Fjords Coloring Books: Color Your Way Int
ISBN-13: 978-0-9971624-2-4
Copyright © 2016 Francis Creek Fjords, LLC, Francis Creek, WI. A...
Published by Francis Creek Fjords (www.FrancisCreekFjords.com). ...

Patti Jo Walter and her husband, Dave Walter, started Francis Creek Fjords (FCF) in 1995. FCF was a Fjord hub for nearly two decades, having Fjords come from all over the United States to be trained, sold on consignment, or bred to their stallion, Fair Acres Ole. Patti Jo began giving riding lessons in 1998, teaching myriad disciplines: huntseat, dressage, jumping, and driving. Today, she continues to instruct dressage and jumping, sharing her passion with anyone wishing to learn and have fun with horses.

Patricia Holland, born and raised in Northeastern Pennsylvania, attended York Academy of Art to pursue a career in commercial art. Dovetailing her lifelong passions of art and horses, she became a professional horse trainer, illustrating what she saw, what she learned, and the people she met along the way. With humor and wit she juggles these contrasting careers, creating a rich and fulfilling life. She resides and illustrates in Galena, Illinois.

Norwegian Fjord Horses (N.F.H.), featured in many of these drawings, are an offshoot horse breed well known for their gentle disposition, calm demeanor, and great versatility, but it's their loving and humorous personalities that draw in most owners. Mutual affection for these charismatic animals caused Pat and Patti's lives to intersect. Once united, Pat's humor and wit served as the perfect complement to Patti's love of life, forging a lifelong friendship in and out of the pasture, much like the horses they admire.

Pat and Patti created this coloring book series as a fun way of learning horseback riding terminology and concepts for Francis Creek Fjords' students. Pat's skillfully drawn illustrations—filled with humor, life, and laughter—combined with Patti's impressive understanding of horses and students resulted in a colorful array of barnyard characters teaching valuable horse-related lessons you can color.

How to use this book

Step 1: Grab your crayons or colored pencils! (Markers are not recommended)

....

Step 2: Choose your favorite picture!

....

Step 3: Color!

....

Step 4: Have fun!

....

Hopefully you enjoy this horse-themed coloring book as much as we enjoyed making it!

A good instructor
will always believe
in you, but you should
still do your best to
make her proud.

So You Want to Find a Good Instructor?

Some Instructors Are Strict ...

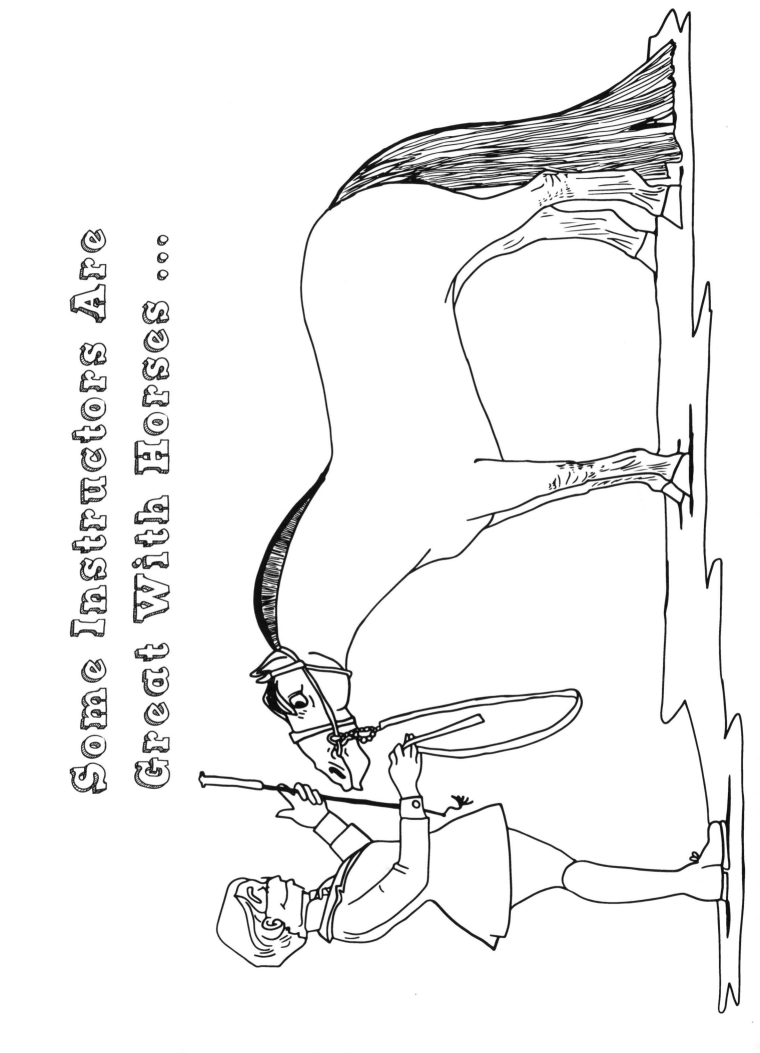

Some Instructors Are Great With Horses ...

A Good Instructor Is Knowledgeable and Patient, and Will Teach You All Sorts of Things

Good Students Trust
Their Instructor!

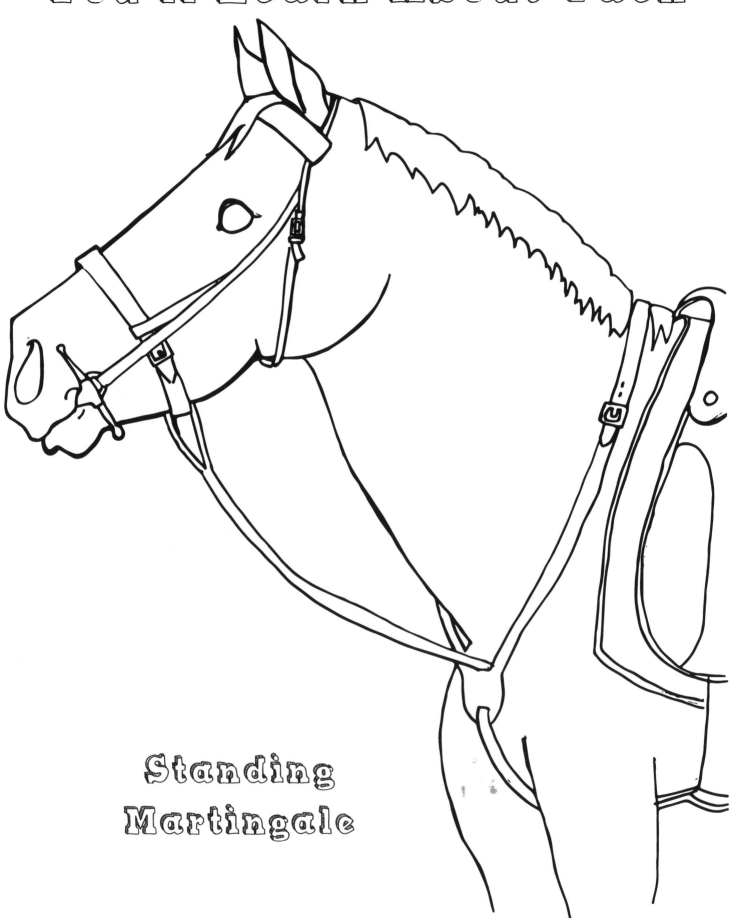

You'll Learn About Tack

Standing
Martingale

Running
Martingale

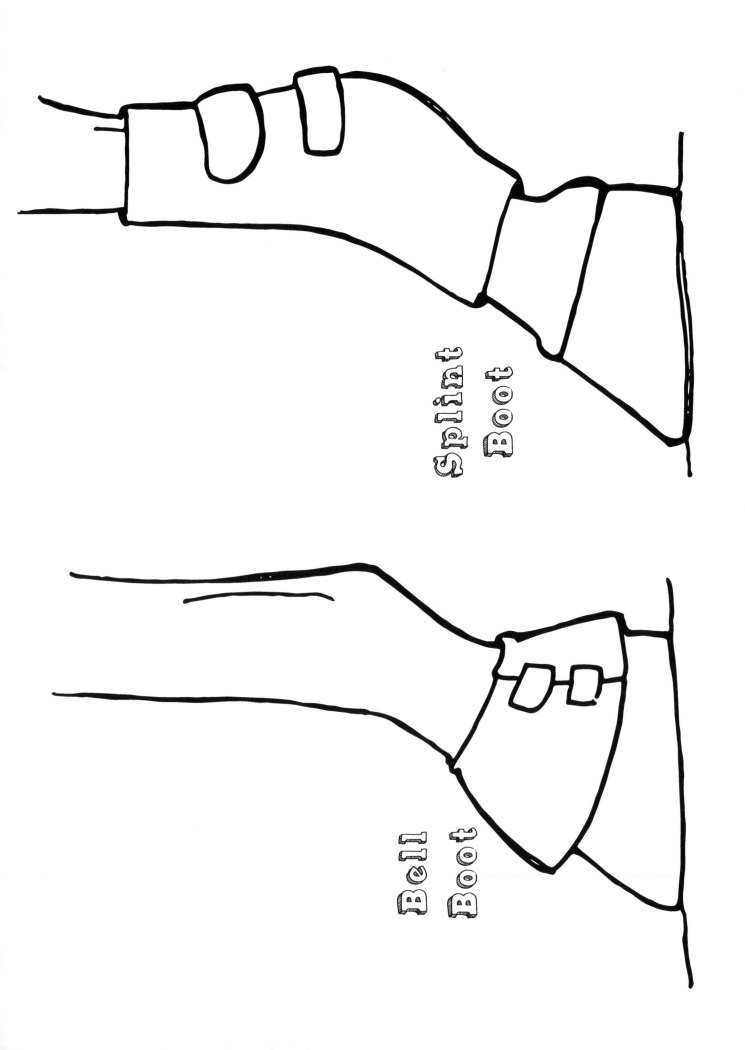

Splint
Boot

Bell
Boot

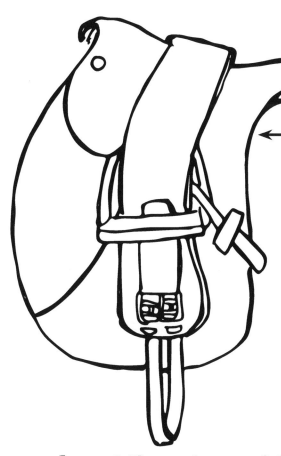

When returning saddle to tack room, irons should be run up and CLEAN, girth slotted from irons. ALWAYS clean and inspect saddles for wear.

A saddle returned to the tack room facing out, depicts a saddle that NEEDS cleaning.

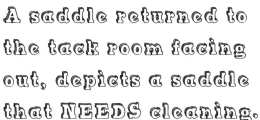

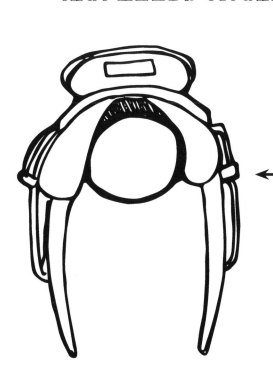

A saddle facing toward the wall NAMEPLATE SHOWN has been cleaned, inspected and ready for use.

Tack Room Etiquette

You'll Learn How to Handle a Horse

Safe, Effective Place to Lead

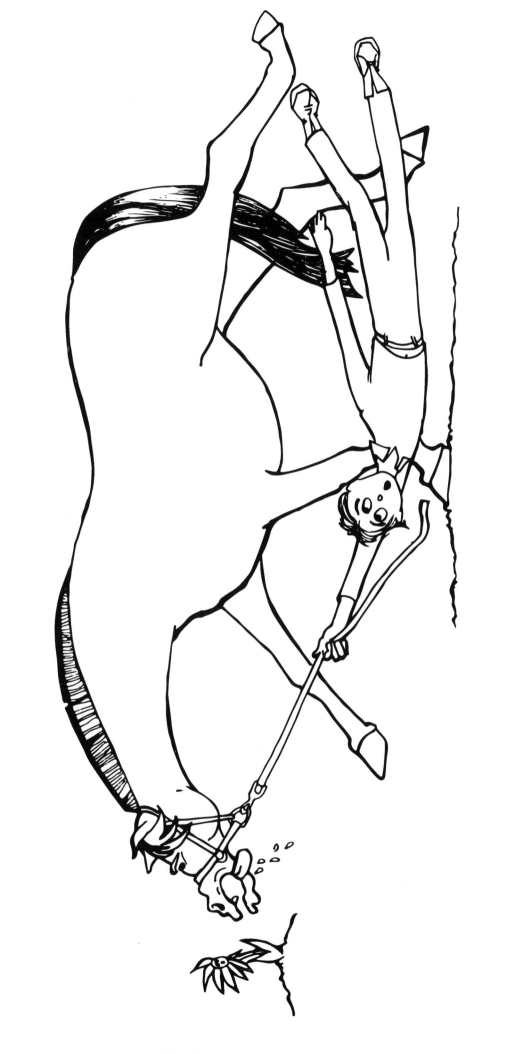

Less Effective Place to Lead ...

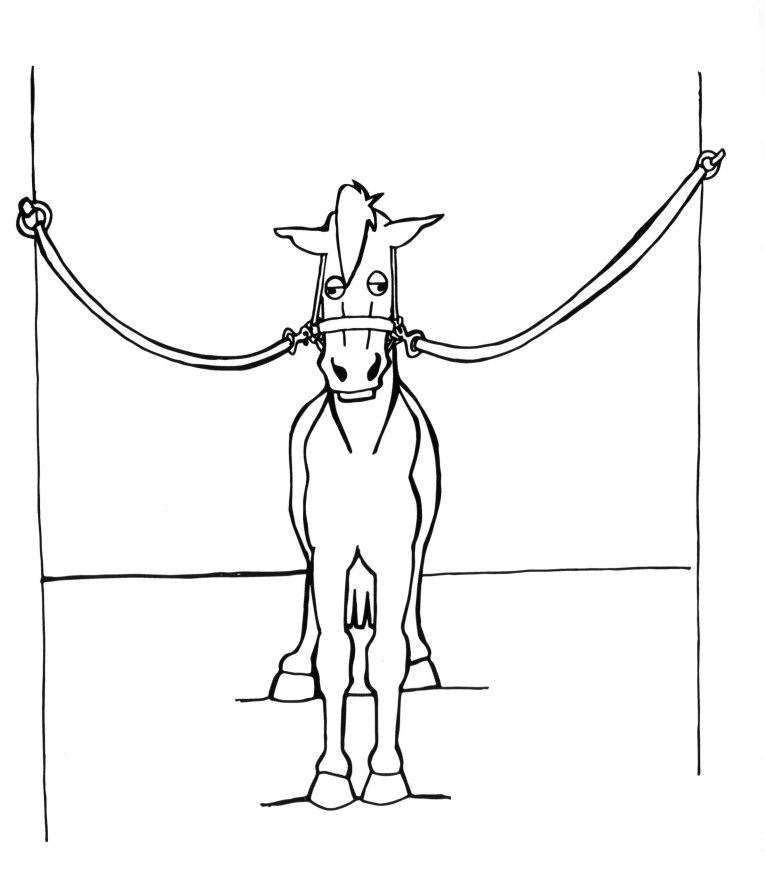

Correct Use of Cross-ties

Cross While Tied

Most Importantly; You'll Learn How to Ride

Introduce the Bit With Confidence

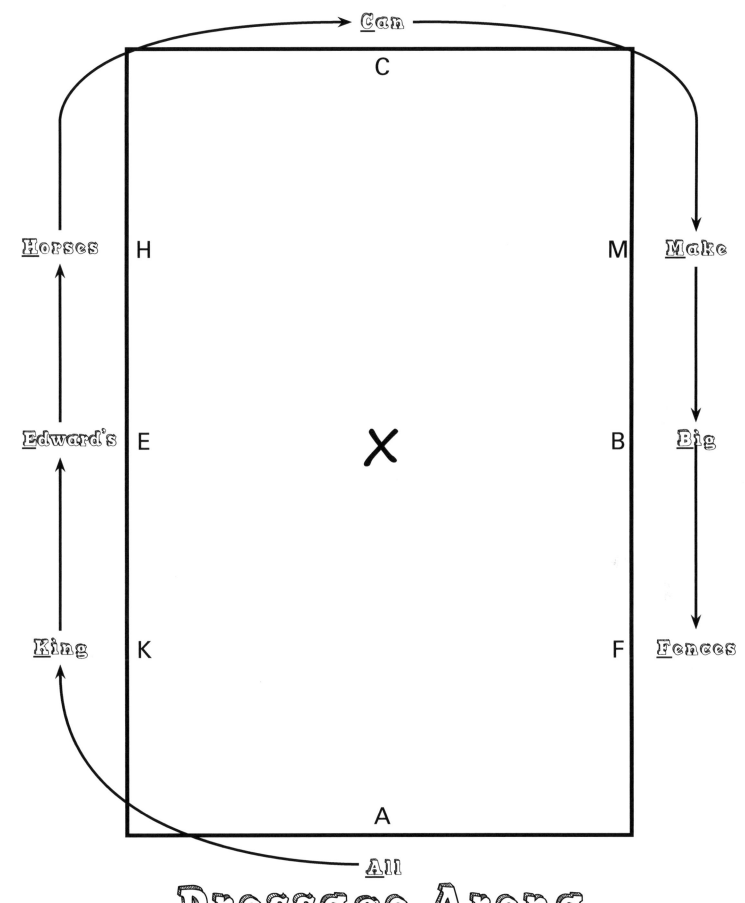

Can

C

Horses H

Edward's E

King K

Make

Big

Fences

M

B

F

X

A

All

Dressage Arena

AKEHCMBF

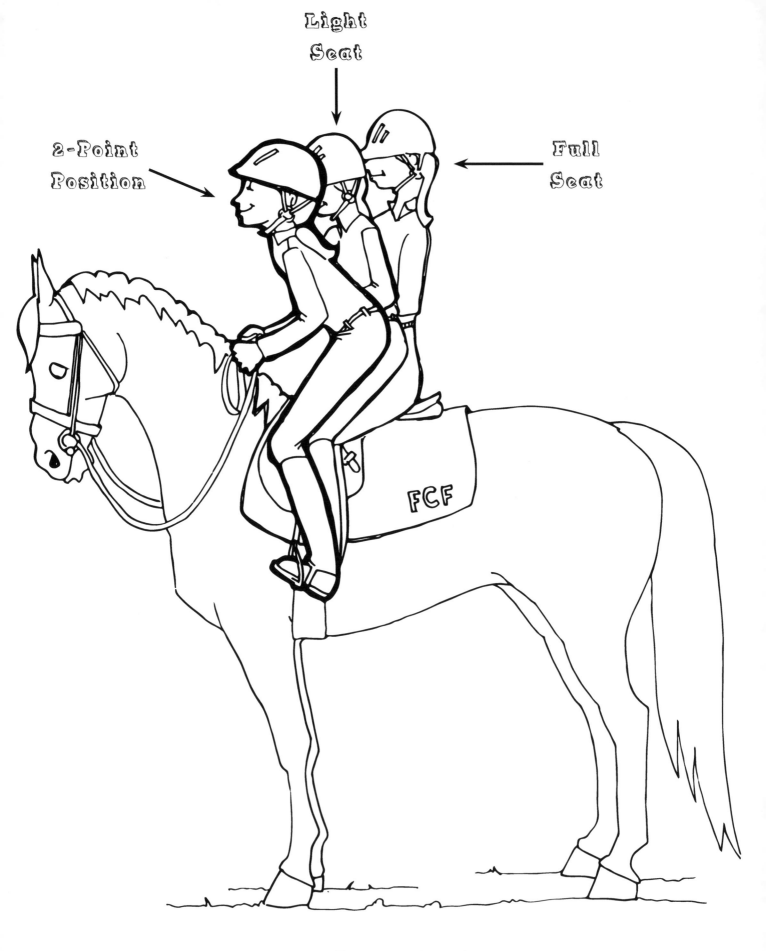

Light
Seat

2-Point
Position

Full
Seat

FCF

Seat Positions

Diagonals

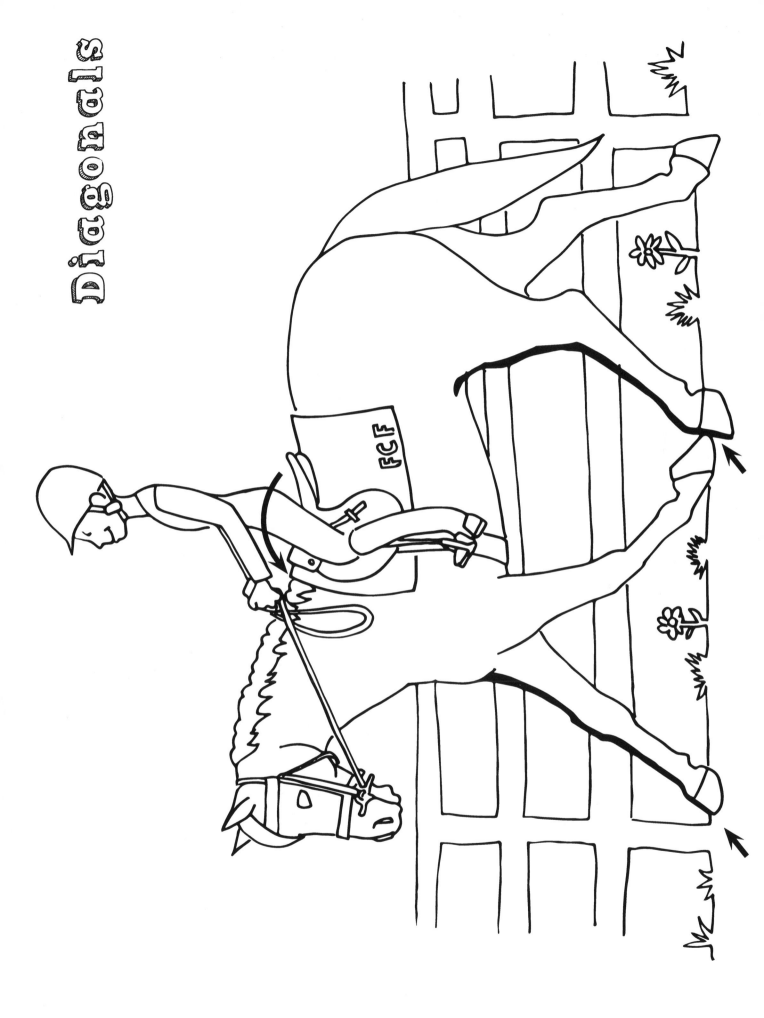

Keep a triangle behind the horse's shoulder

You'll Learn About Your Horse

Lunging is the perfect
way to OBSERVE your horse.
To SEE how your horse moves.
To SEE his abilities and weaknesses.
To take the edge off.
To teach voice commands.

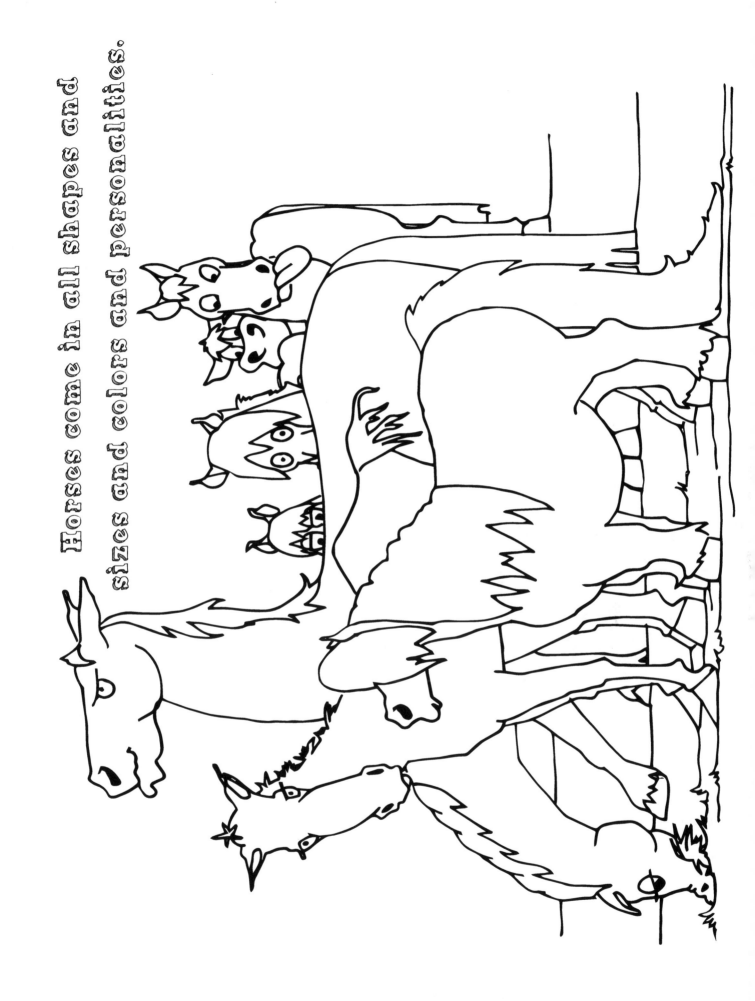

Horses come in all shapes and sizes and colors and personalities.

Gaited Horses

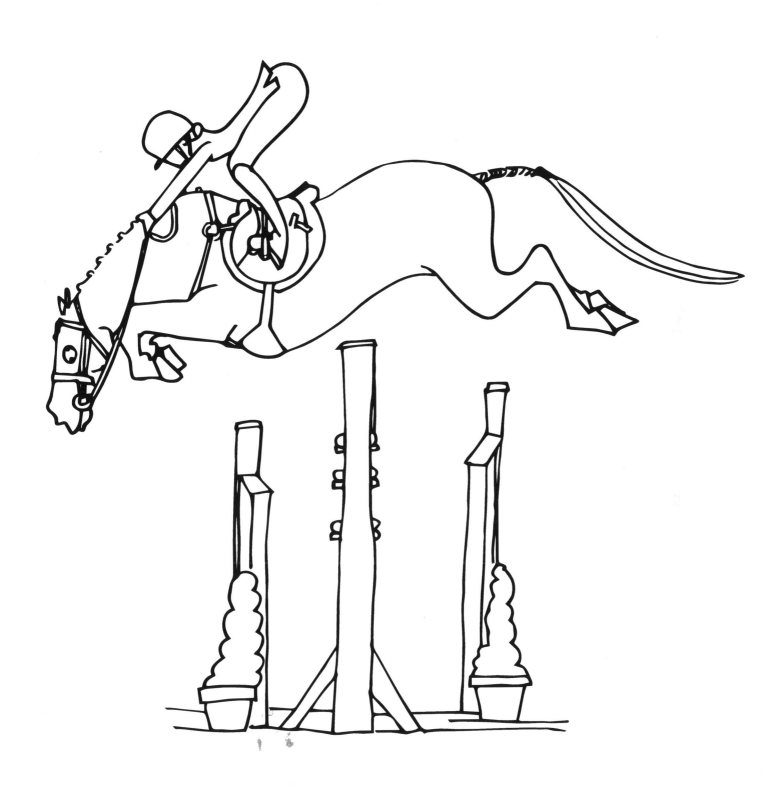

Jumping Horses

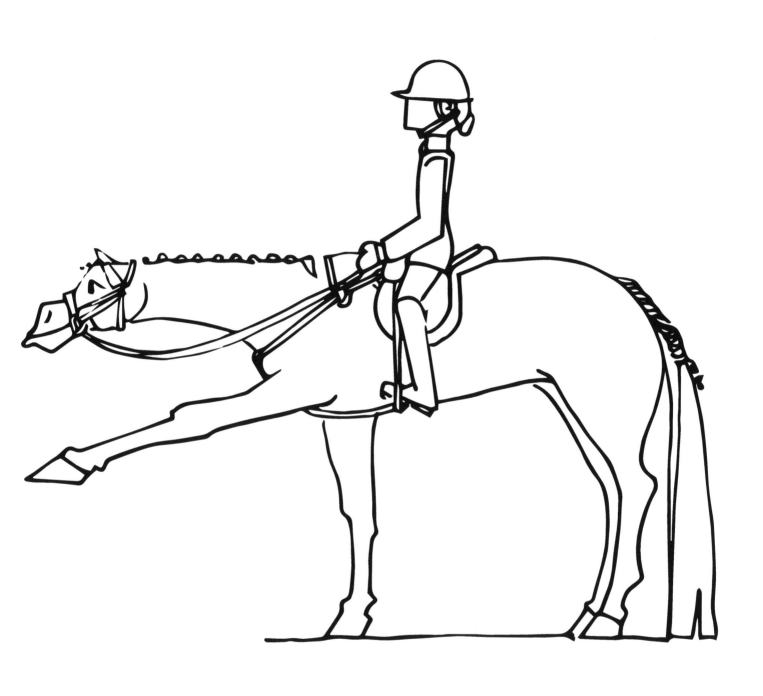

Hunter Horses

Western Pleasure Horses

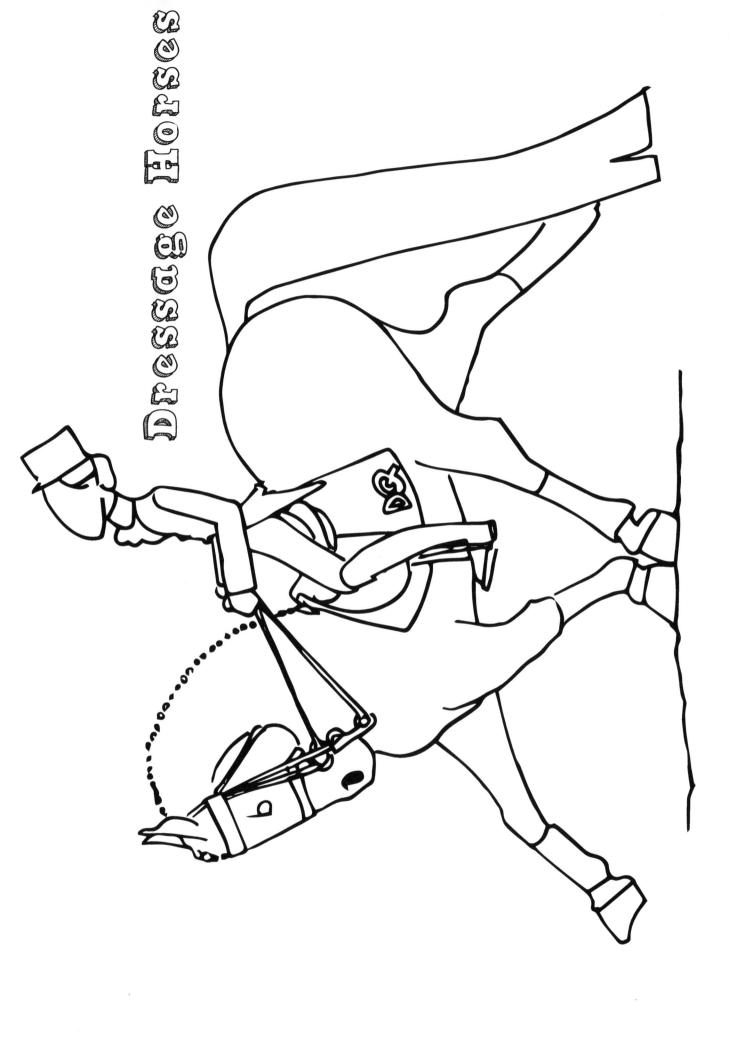

and Driving Horses

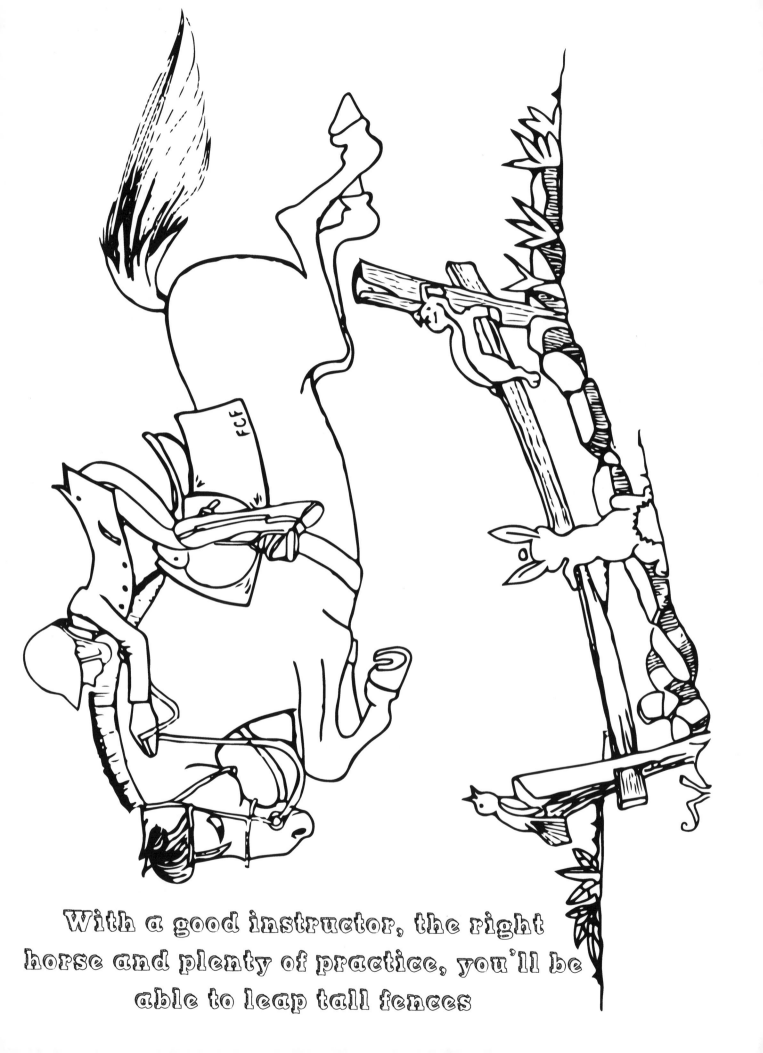

With a good instructor, the right horse and plenty of practice, you'll be able to leap tall fences

Fun Fjord Fact: Many people believe all Fjords are fat. In reality, they're big-boned and big-muscled, but leave a Fjord in a lush pasture and it'll eat all day.

We're always working on new books!
Write to us (fcfwalter@gmail.com) with
your comments, ideas, or suggestions.

Francis Creek Fjords Coloring Books

Color Your Way Into
English Riding 1

By Patti Jo Walter and Pat Holland

You might also like:

Color Your Way Into English Riding 1!

Color Your Way Into Western Riding!

Francis Creek Fjords Coloring Books

Color Your Way Into
Western Riding

By Patti Jo Walter and Pat Holland

and ...

Color Your Way Into a Horse for Christmas!

Francis Creek Fjords Coloring **Books**

Color Your Way Into

A Horse for Christmas

By Patti Jo Walter and Pat Holland

Made in the USA
San Bernardino, CA
12 February 2019